Reading Plus Comprehension

1

Ruth Lewis

Illustrated by Celina Korcak

Reading Plus Comprehension 1

Text: Ruth Lewis
Illustrations: Celina Korcak
Text design: Modern Art Production
Cover design: James Lowe
Production Controller: Hanako Smith

Reading Plus Comprehension

For product information and technology assistance,
in Australia call 1300 790 853;
in New Zealand call 0508 635 766

For permission to use material from this text or product,
please email **aust.permissions@cengage.com**

ISBN 978 0 17 012300 6

Cengage Learning Australia
Level 7, 80 Dorcas Street
South Melbourne, Victoria Australia 3205

Cengage Learning New Zealand
Unit 4B Rosedale Office Park
331 Rosedale Road, Albany, North Shore NZ 0632

For learning solutions, visit **cengage.com.au**

Printed in China by 1010 Printing International Limited
9 10 11 25 24 23 22 21 20

Contents

About this Book

For Teachers

Reading Plus Comprehension 1 is a comprehension workbook comprising forty-nine units graded in difficulty, for use in the first year of primary school. The steadily increasing complexity of language, concepts, exercises and questions reflects the growing skills of students throughout the school year. For this reason, students should progress through the workbook in a systematic rather than a random fashion. As their competence increases, students will progress from pictorial representation to the written word.

Each unit in *Reading Plus Comprehension* is thematic, focusing on the life experiences of five- and six-year-olds, and links to the key learning areas in the curriculum. The comprehension questions in the workbook are a mixture of literal and inferential.

- **Literal questions** ask students to find specific information in the text and/or illustrations, to select correct information from a number of alternatives or to determine the truth of statements about the text and/or illustrations.
- **Inferential questions** ask students to link meaning with other sources of information either in or beyond the text.

Each unit has definite outcomes that will develop children's reading and comprehension skills and bring meaning and understanding to language and writing at a personal level.

Reading Plus Comprehension includes a full set of answers, and a checklist for key learning areas is located at the back of the book so that individual student progress may be monitored.

Reading Plus Comprehension lends itself both to group and individual work in the classroom. Icons are shown in each unit as indicators to identify the appropriate focus. It is not intended that students work on the units without prior preparation; in order to gain maximum advantage from the workbook, the class should read and discuss the exercises before students begin individual work on the questions. The class can then come together to discuss the answers to questions and to share responses.

Group work

Child to work alone

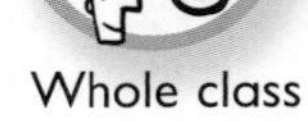

Whole class

For Parents

Parents are also responsible for introducing language to their children. You play an important part in your child's schooling, so your children need your time and encouragement. *Reading Plus Comprehension* enables you, as a parent, to assist your child in developing essential reading and comprehension skills.

When using this workbook bear in mind that comprehension is not a test of a child's memory; it is a way of developing their understanding of written text. Always encourage your child to search the text for answers. Be aware that children often make mistakes in comprehension because they do not understand what they are reading. Read the text with your child and help them with the meanings of unfamiliar words.

Using the *Reading Plus Comprehension* series, you and your child's teacher can work together to give your child confidence in his or her own ability and understanding of language, reading and writing.

Cross Curricular Links Overview

Unit	Theme	Objective	Literacy	Maths	Social Studies	Science and Technology	Personal Development	Creative Arts
1	How Many Legs?	Classifies the animals correctly	•			•		
2	What's Missing	Locates the missing part of each object. Draws them, where they belong	•	•				•
3	Humpty Dumpty	Discusses both rhyme and pictures. Traces, and then colours them. Locates differences in all pictures	•			•		•
4	Sounds	Follows the directions to identify objects that don't make a sound	•		•	•		
5	Reading	Reads then draws pictures. Completes a sentence	•			•		
6	Family	Traces words, then follows the directions to colour pictures. Sequences the words for sentences, then writes them	•	•	•			•
7	Alphabet	Writes name, then draws self. Traces all letters in the blocks. Draws a friend, writes their name	•				•	•
8	Living, Non-Living	Follows the directions to identify both living and non-living things	•		•	•		
9	Hey Diddle Diddle	Sequences events in the rhyme. Reads/traces words, then matches them to pictures	•		•	•		•
10	The Kitchen	Matches objects in picture to pictures below	•		•			•
11	Safety	Draws the icon beneath each unsafe article	•			•	•	
12	Colours	Traces 'red' and 'yellow', then colours these objects correctly	•		•			•
13	What Doesn't Belong?	Marks the objects that do not belong in each set	•		•			•
14	Seasons	Talks about two seasons, traces their names. Identifies autumn colours, then colours both pictures	•			•		•
15	The Senses – Touch	Identifies different attributes for hot, cold, soft and hard	•	•	•	•		•
16	More Words	Matches words and pictures, then traces these words. Follows the directions to colour pictures	•		•			•
17	The Gingerbread Man	Reads rhyme, and then traces the Gingerbread Man. Reads picture story, then traces words. Predicts the next event, then writes story and illustrates it	•		•		•	•
18	Party Time	Discusses party hats, then marks favourite one. Writes names of three friends to invite to a party	•	•	•		•	•
19	Painting the House	Identifies all objects that don't belong in picture. Follows directions to colour in	•		•			•
20	Fruit	Locates sets by their colour. Completes a sentence	•		•			•
21	Three Blind Mice	Sequences pictures correctly. Matches rhyming words with pictures	•	•	•			•
22	Stripes and Spots	Follows instructions to identify animals that do not belong in each set	•			•		•
23	Nursery Rhymes	Orders the pictures to match the rhyme. Writes sentences to match pictures	•	•	•			•
24	Clothes	Classifies the correct sets of clothing	•			•		•
25	On the Grass	Matches objects in picture to pictures below	•			•		•

Cross Curricular Links Overview

Unit	Theme	Objective	Literacy	Maths	Social Studies	Science and Technology	Personal Development	Creative Arts
26	Position	Discusses the front/back views of pictures, then matches them. Colours as directed	•	•				•
27	Car Trips	Discusses family outings. Marks the places where they have been by car. Draws family at the snow/at the beach	•		•			•
28	Hickory Dickory Dock	Sequences pictures correctly. Traces, and then completes the story				•		•
29	Up and Down	Matches animals' and people's movements	•	•		•		•
30	The Birthday Card	Traces writing. Talks about the party. Predicts the next scene and draws the picture	•		•	•		•
31	Words and Pictures	Colours matching words and pictures. Reads the sentence, traces word, and then draws it	•					•
32	Spring	Completes the picture as instructed	•		•	•		•
33	What Are They Going to Do?	Predicts which picture will match the one in the box. Completes each sentence	•		•			•
34	The Little Red Hen	Discusses the story, then traces the words. Numbers the boxes correctly	•			•	•	•
35	Things That Move	Colours the things that move in a similar way. Labels pictures, then traces words	•		•	•		•
36	Colours	Identifies objects that are the same colour	•		•	•		•
37	Ducks	Discusses, then reads story. Traces words. Matches words and pictures. Colours objects that don't belong	•			•		•
38	Time	Traces the words, then colours pictures	•		•	•		•
39	Telephones	Circles the people who might ring. Traces words then writes conversations in the speech bubbles	•	•			•	•
40	Feelings	Identifies people's feelings. Follows instructions to complete activity	•				•	•
41	More Words and Pictures	Colours words and matching pictures. Traces word. Reads sentence, then draws picture	•					•
42	Books	Predicts story by looking at cover. Names books, then colours objects that belong to each book	•		•			•
43	Weather	Matches 'weather' words to class weather chart. Writes words as instructed	•			•		
44	At Home	Matches objects. Colours objects that need a key	•			•	•	
45	Fishing	Finds objects that do not belong	•		•			
46	The Fire Engine	Discusses pictures and reads words, then answers questions	•				•	•
47	The Race	Talks about sports day at a school that caters for disabled children	•				•	•
48	Traditional Stories	Identifies the characters that belong in each book	•					•
49	Little Boy Blue	Uses the word bank to help name each picture. Sequences pictures. Follows instructions to complete picture	•		•	•		•

Identification

Colour the animals in each row that belong together.

Categories

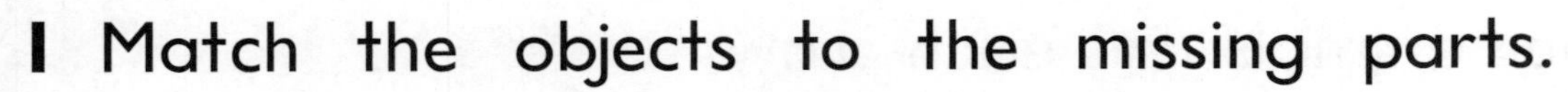

1 Match the objects to the missing parts.

2 Draw, then colour the finished objects.

Poem

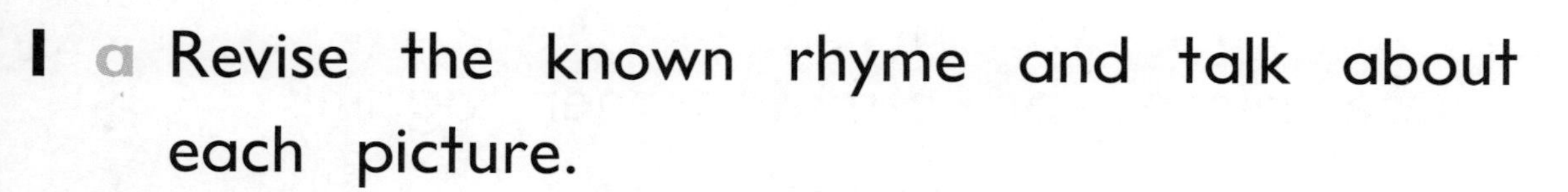

1 a Revise the known rhyme and talk about each picture.

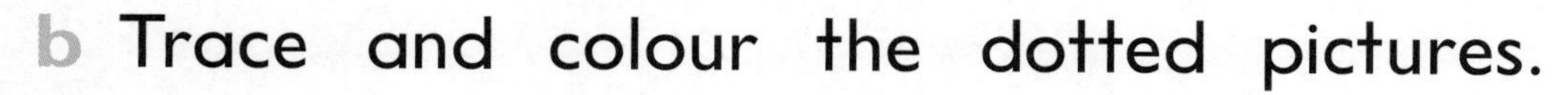

b Trace and colour the dotted pictures.

c Draw yourself looking at Humpty.

Inference

2 Can these pieces be put together again? Write 'yes' or 'no' for each one.

a ______ b ______ c ______

3 Draw a cross on the picture that is different in each row.

Classification

1 Colour any object that does not make a sound.

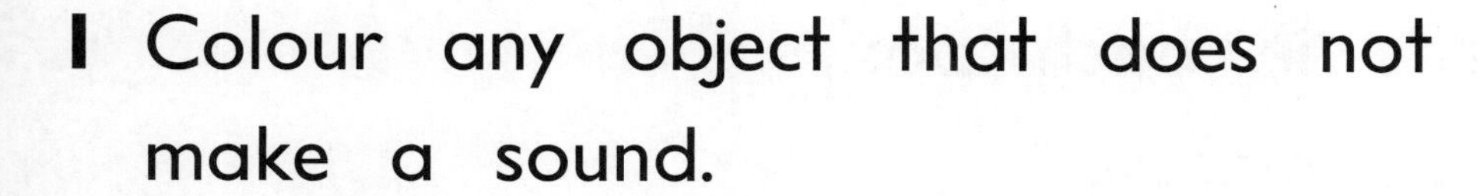

2 Put a cross on any object that does not make a sound.

3 Circle any object that does not make a sound.

4 Draw a box around any object that does not make a sound.

Description

1 Read the words in each box, then draw each picture.

a	b
a black cat	a big tree

c	d
Mum and Dad	a little mouse

2 Complete the sentence and colour the picture.

I can see a ______________________.

Description

I a Trace each word then write it below.
b Colour the cat orange and the kitten black.
c Colour the chair yellow.

Mum

big

little

cat

Sequence

2 Read these words, then write them as sentences.

a Mum My big is.

b little is cat My.

3 Draw a picture of a cat or a dog.

Description

1 a Write your name on the line.
b Draw a picture of yourself.
c Trace the letters and colour the blocks.

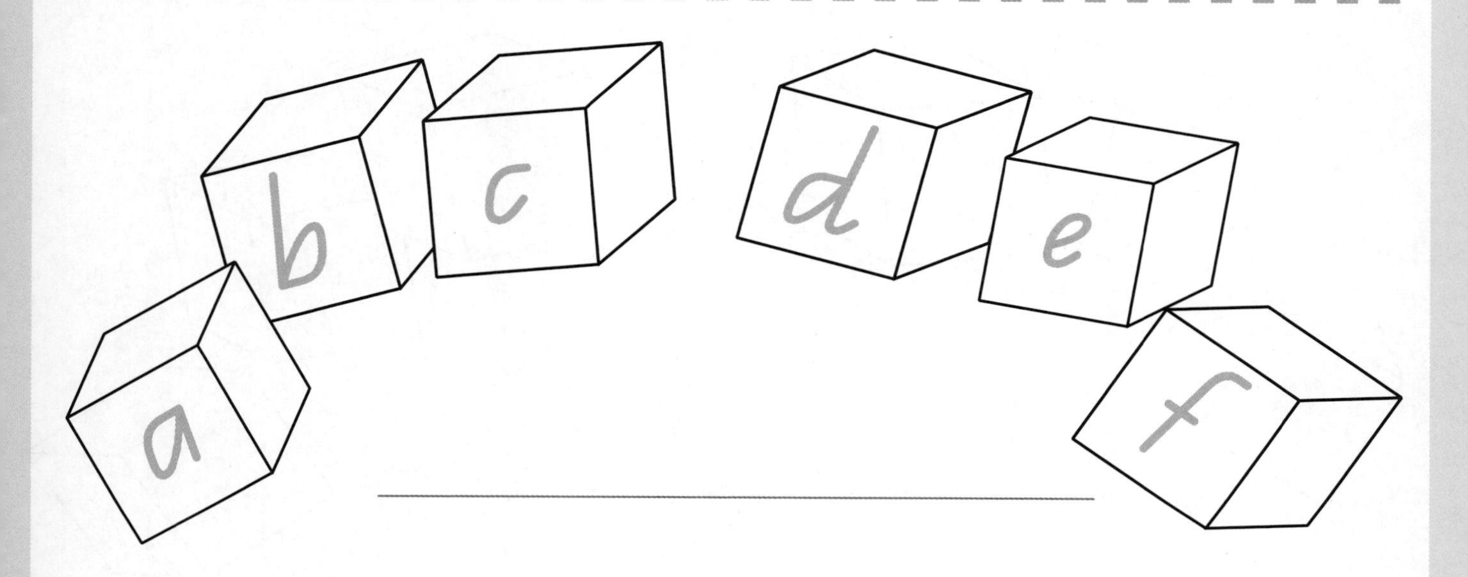

Description

2 a Draw your friend and write their name.
b Write what you like about your friend.
c Trace the letters and colour the blocks.

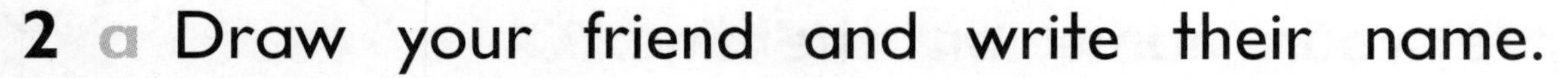

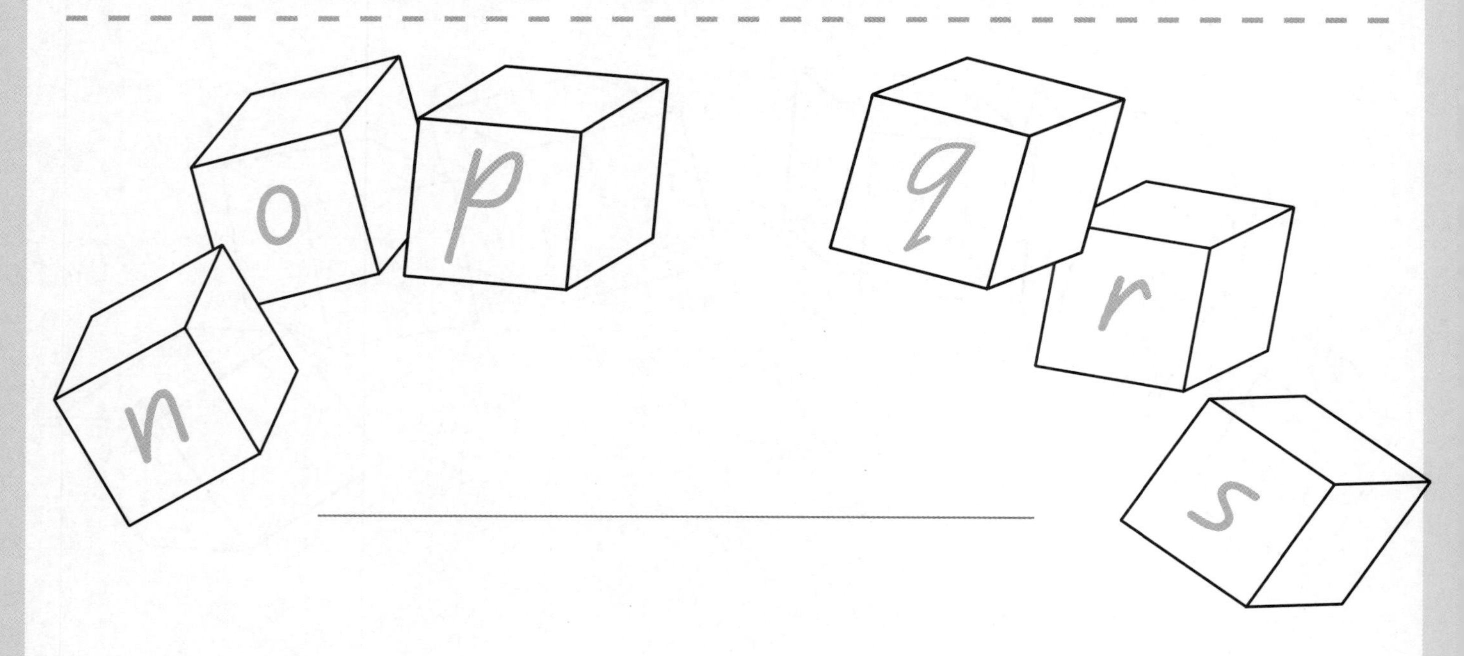

I like

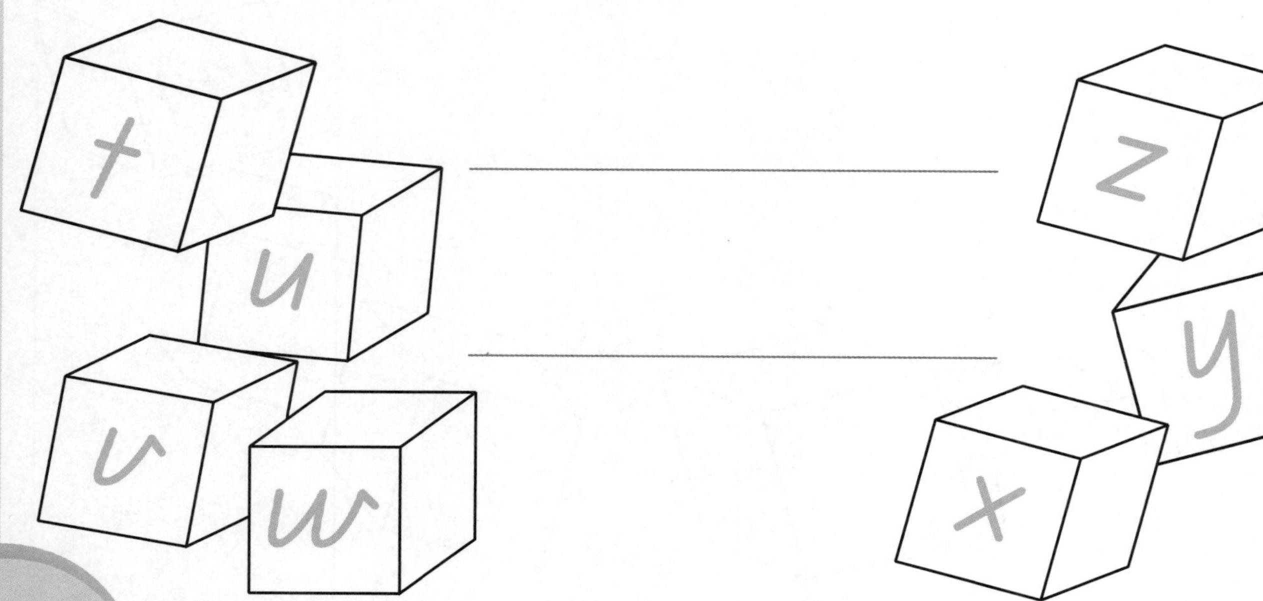

Classification

1 a Colour all the living things.

b Circle all the non-living things.

Sequence

1 Order the events by numbering the boxes 1 – 4.

2 Read and trace the words, then match them to the pictures.

a

cat

b

dish

c

cow

d

dog

Identification

1 a Put a tick in each box as you find the object in the picture.

b Colour the picture.

Instruction

1 a Talk about the meaning of the symbol.

b Draw the symbol in the circle below each unsafe object.

Identification

1 a Trace the word.

b Use a red pencil to colour all the objects that should be red.

2 a Trace the word.

b Use a yellow pencil to colour all the objects that should be yellow.

Categories

1 Put a cross on the object that does not belong in each row, then colour the ones left.

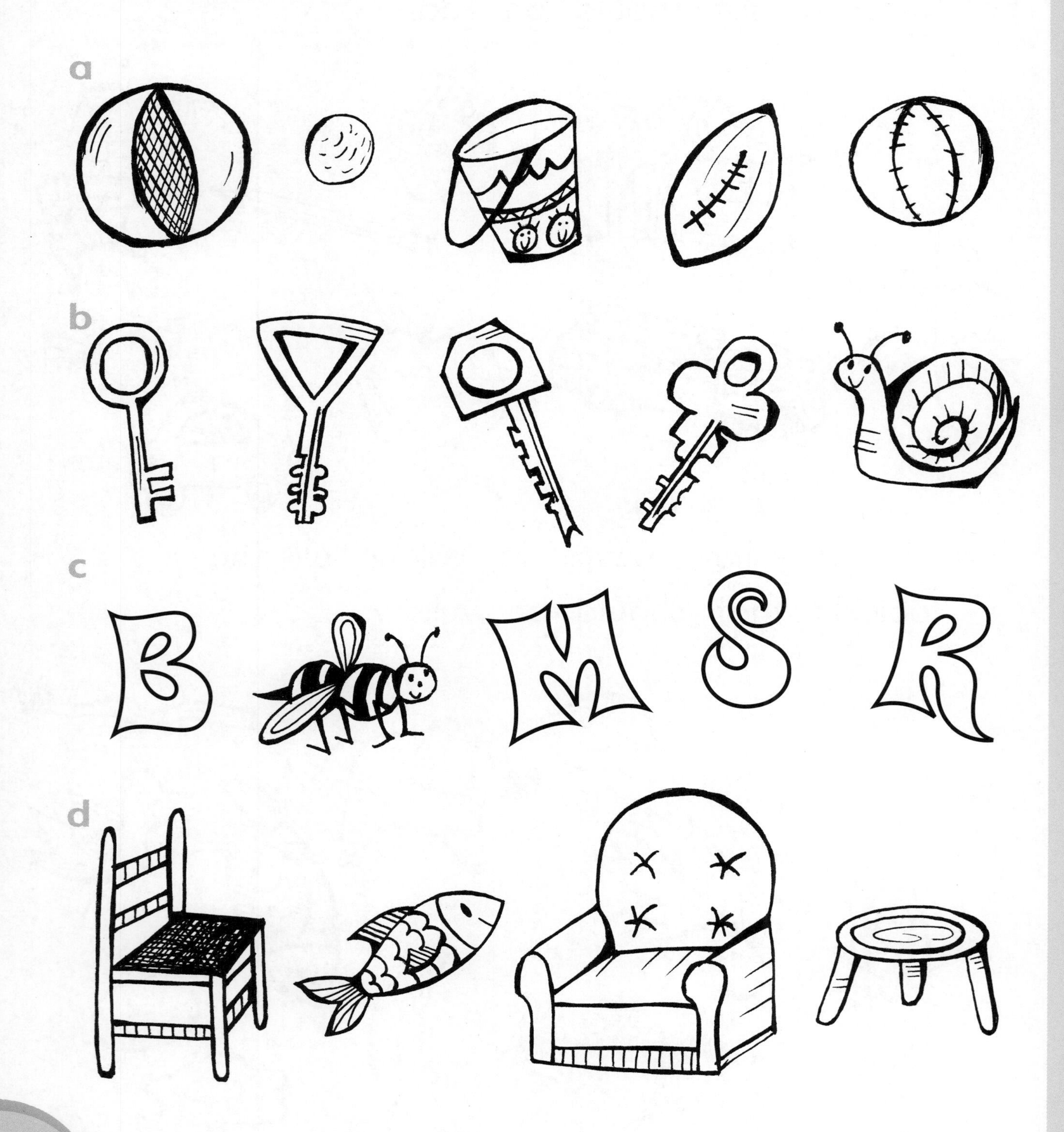

Description

1 Talk about Autumn and Winter.

2 a Trace the word.

b Colour the leaves red, green, brown and yellow.

Autumn

3 a Trace the word.

b Colour the picture.

Winter

Classification

1 Colour all the hot things.

2 Put a cross on all the cold things.

3 Circle all the soft things.

4 Draw a box around all the hard things.

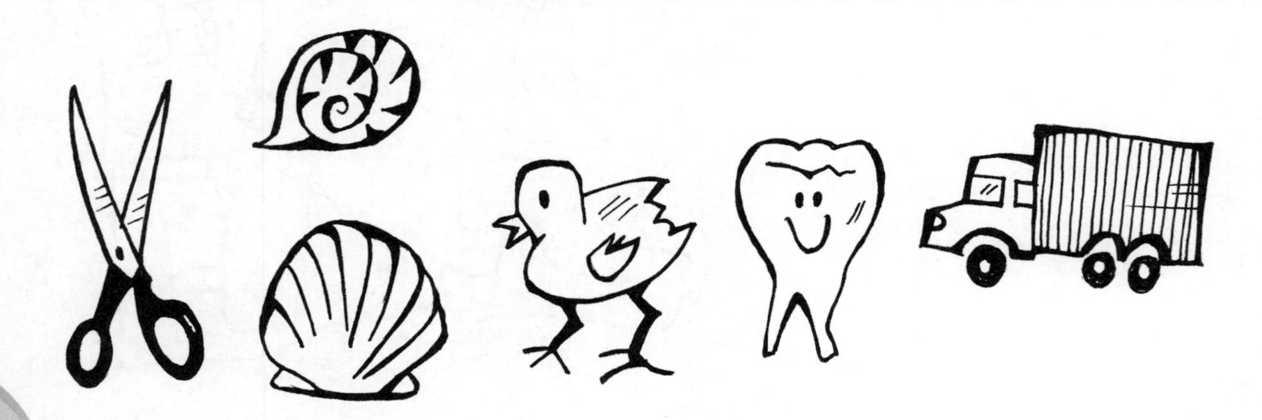

Description

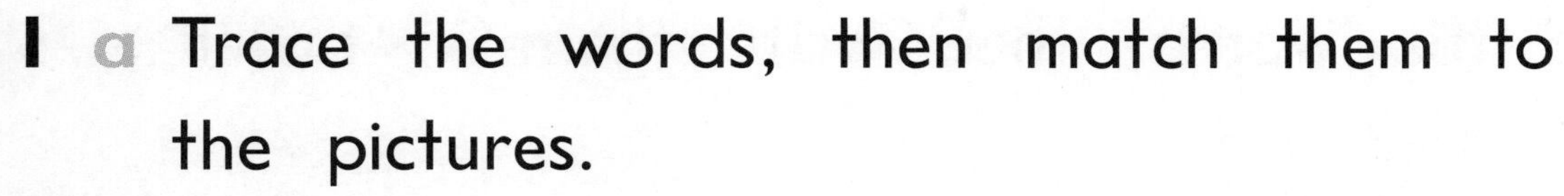

1 a Trace the words, then match them to the pictures.

b Put black spots on the puppy, then colour Dad's shirt and jeans.

Order

2 a Read the words, then write them in order as a sentence.

b Draw a picture.

to runs dog A Dad.

____

3 a Write a sentence using the words **girl** and **little**.

b Draw the picture.

girl little She a is.

____

Poem

1 a Read the rhyme.

b Trace the Gingerbread Man and colour him.

Run, run, run
as fast as you can.
You can't catch me.
I'm the Gingerbread Man.

Narrative

2 Read the picture story.

3 Trace the words.

dog cow fox

4 Draw and write down what happened next.

Matching

1 Draw a line from each present to the correct parcel. Be careful!

Instruction

2 Put a tick on the party hat you like.
Colour the other party hats.

3 Write the names of three friends
you would invite to your party.

____

____

____

4 Draw candles on the cake
to show how old you are.

Categories

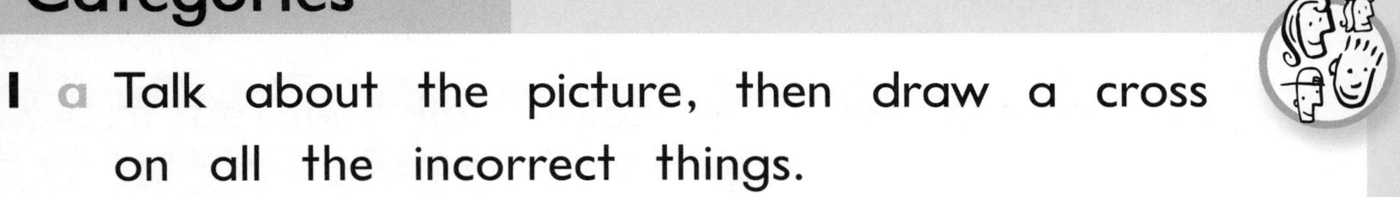

1 a Talk about the picture, then draw a cross on all the incorrect things.

b Colour the giraffe orange, the man's shirt blue and the house yellow.

Description

1 a Use a red pencil to colour all the red fruit.

b Circle all the yellow fruit, then colour them.

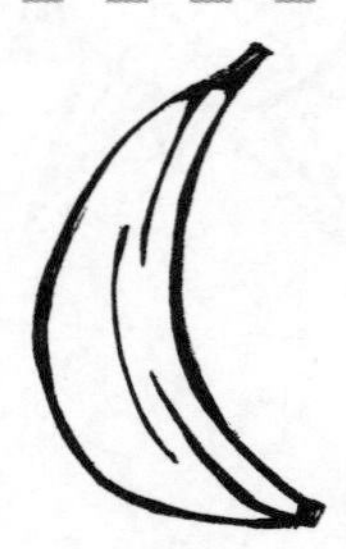
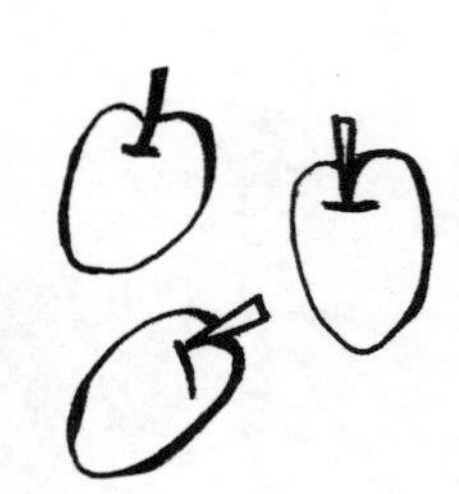

c Draw a box around all the green fruit, then colour them.

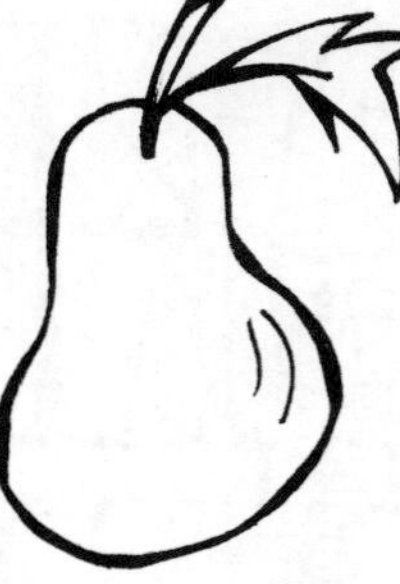

2 Finish the sentence about food you like to eat.

I like to eat ______________________________

____

Selection

1 a Choose the correct word from the word bank to write under each picture.

b Colour the rhyming pictures in each row.

Word bank

mice
dice
rice
hose

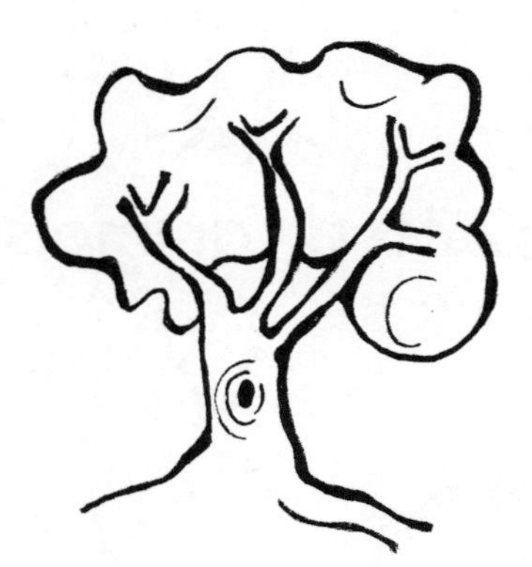

Word bank

three
tree
toe
bee

Word bank

run
mum
sun
bun

Description

1 Colour the animals that move slowly.

   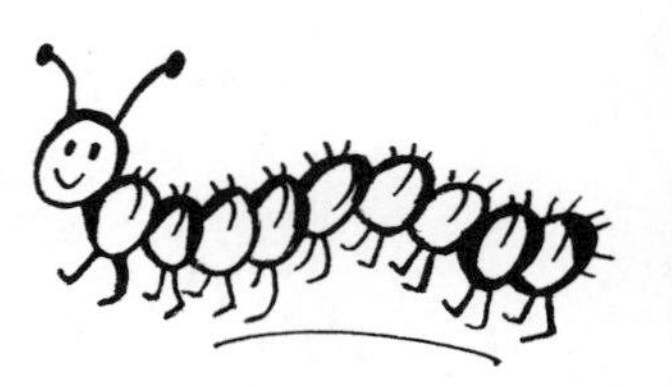

2 Circle the animals that move fast.

3 Put a cross on the spotted animals.

4 Draw a box around the striped animals.

Identification

5 Draw red spots on the slow animal.
Draw coloured stripes on the fast animals.
Use the word bank to help you name each animal.

____

____

______________ ______________

Word bank

turtle
dog
emu
tiger

6 Draw stripes on the animals starting with 'c'.

cat

penguin

cow

camel

Sequence

1 Order the pictures by numbering the boxes 1 – 4.

2 Colour the mice brown with pink ears, and give the farmer's wife a yellow top and blue jeans.

a

b

c

d

Sequence

3 Order the pictures by numbering the boxes 1 – 4.

4 Colour the sheep black.

5 Number the bags of wool in picture d.

a

b

c

d

Description

4 Select the best sentence for each picture and write it below.

a

b

c

d

I am the farmer. I am the little boy.

I am the dame. I am the black sheep.

Classification

1 Circle the object that doesn't belong in each row.

Instruction

1 a Tick each box as you find the object in the picture.

b Colour the picture.

Identification

1 Match the front and back of each object.

2 Colour the front of the car blue, the man's hair brown, the teddy bear orange, and the clock face red.

Recount

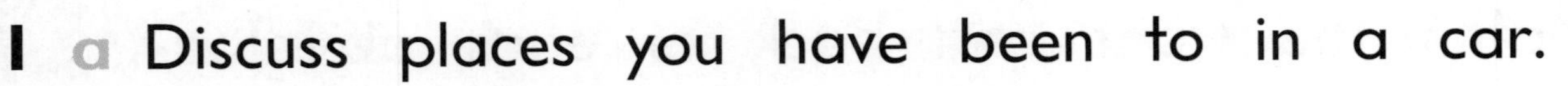

1 a Discuss places you have been to in a car.

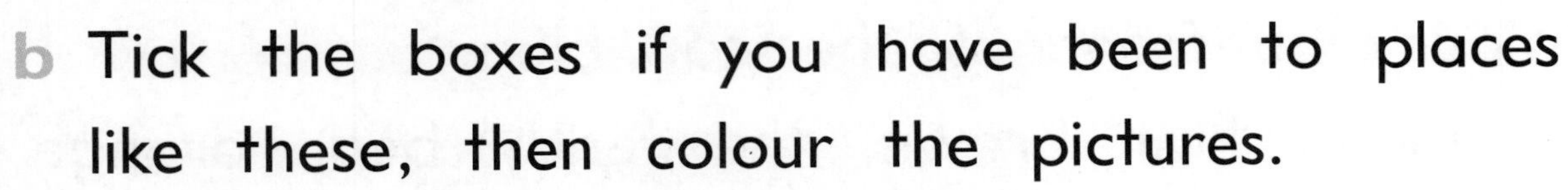

b Tick the boxes if you have been to places like these, then colour the pictures.

2 Draw your family at both of these places.

at the snow

at the beach

Order

1 a Order the pictures 1 – 3.

b Colour the mouse in each picture brown with pink ears and a red nose.

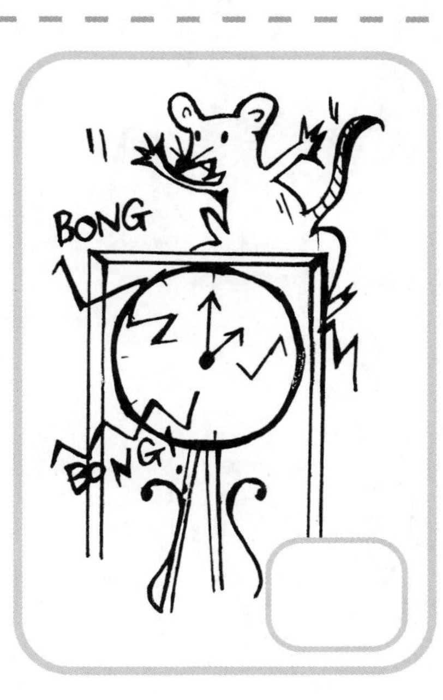

2 a Trace the number 1.

b Complete the sentence.

1 A mouse ran

Categories

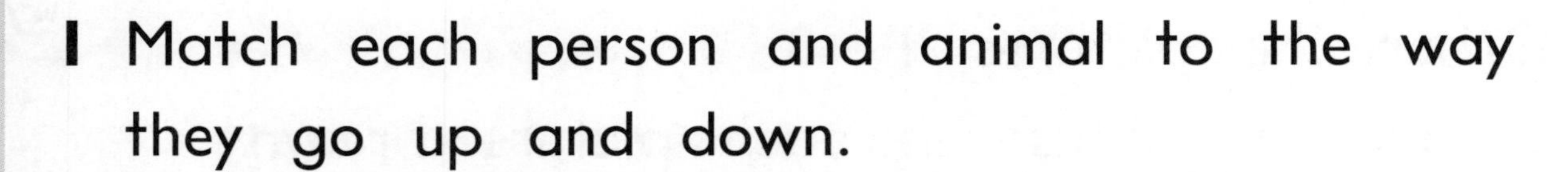

1 Match each person and animal to the way they go up and down.

2 Put a cross on everything that can climb up and down. Colour the pictures.

Tracing

1 a Trace the birthday card greetings.

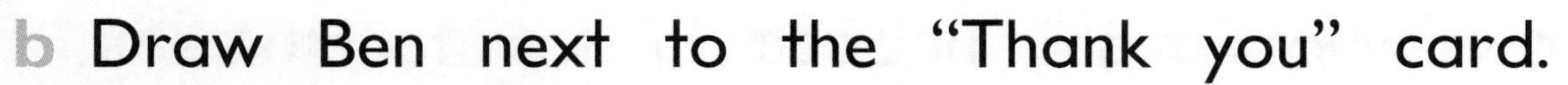

b Draw Ben next to the "Thank you" card.

Ben
10 Tapp St
Toyland
1555

Happy
birthday,
Ben

Prediction

2 Talk about what is happening in each picture.

3 Draw what might happen in the fourth box.

Description

1 Colour the picture to match the word in each box.

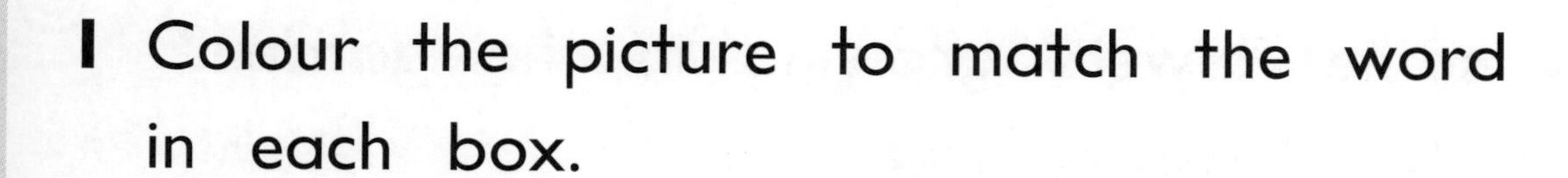

2 Read the sentence, trace **pig** and draw a picture.

Look at the pig.

Instruction

1 a Draw some flowers growing in the garden.
  b Colour the blossom tree pink.
  c Draw red spots on one girl's clothes and blue stripes on the other girl's clothes.

Prediction

1 Colour the pictures that match.

a

b

c

d

Prediction

2 These two children are going to school.
Draw your school.

3 Where are these children going?
Colour the correct picture.
Use the word bank to help you.

a The boy is running
for a ___ ___ ___ .

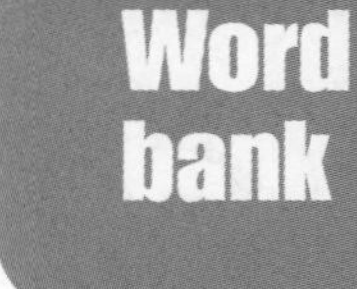

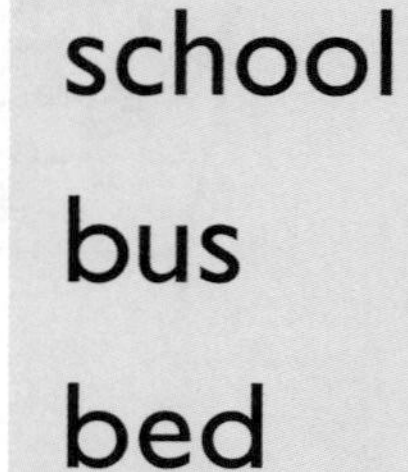

school
bus
bed

b The girl is going to
___ ___ ___ ___ ___ ___ .

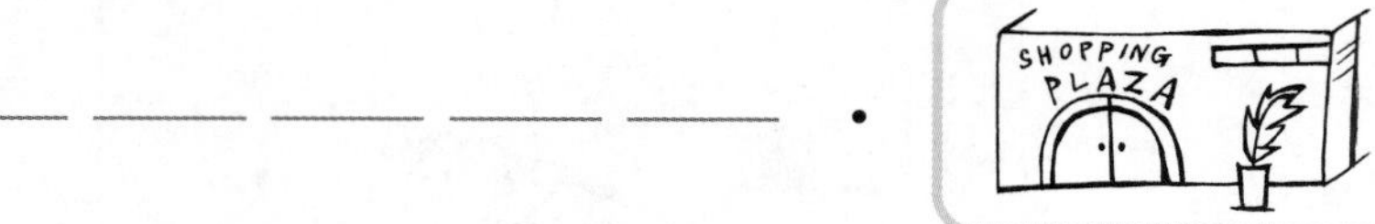

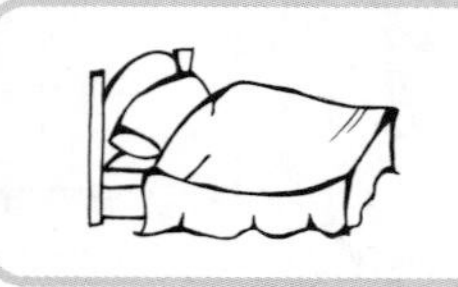

c The boy is going to
___ ___ ___ .

Narrative

I a Read and talk about the story.
b Trace the words.

"Who will help me plant this seed?" said the Little Red Hen.

"Not I," said the dog.

"Not I," said the cat.

"Not I," said the pig.

"Well, I shall do it myself."
And she did.

Sequence

2 Order these pictures by numbering the boxes correctly.

3 Put a tick in the box if these animals helped the little red hen. Trace the words.

cat dog pig

4 Draw the Little Red Hen eating her cakes, then trace the word **hen**.

hen

Classification

1 Colour all the things in each row that move in the same way.

2 Draw a red bus.

Instruction

3 a Label the pictures with words from the word bank.

b Colour the things with wheels.

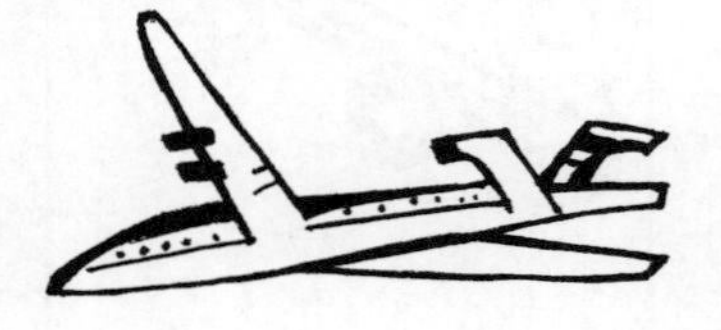

Word bank

van
car
jet
boat
train
bus

4 Trace the rocket, then add the moon and three stars.

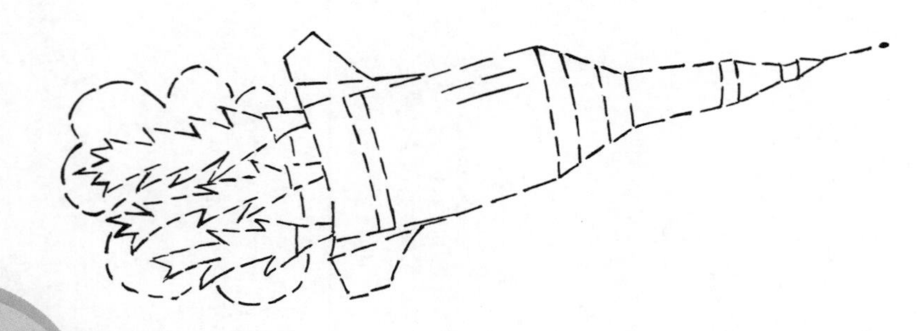

Association

1 Put a cross on the objects that are the same colour as the object in the box. Colour them correctly.

Description

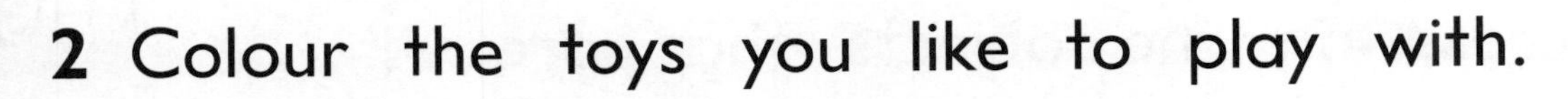

2 Colour the toys you like to play with.

3 Draw:

a red hen	a yellow duck	a blue hat

Narrative

I a Read and talk about the story.

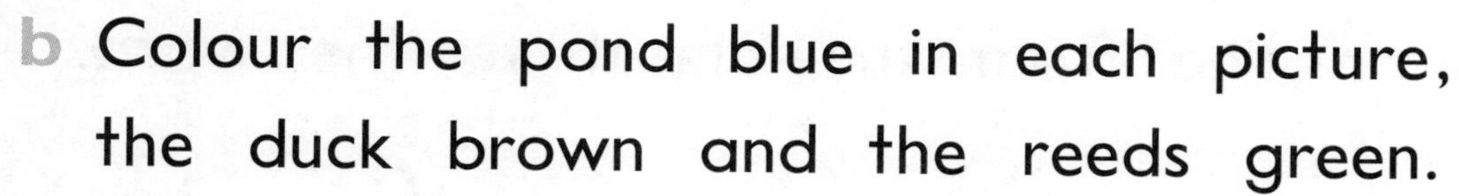

b Colour the pond blue in each picture, the duck brown and the reeds green.

c Draw a fish in the duck's mouth in the last picture.

Here is a duck.

The duck is in the water.

Where is the duck?

The duck has a fish.

Description

2 a Trace the three words.

b Draw a line from the object to the word.

water

fish

duck

3 Colour the ducks that are exactly the same.

4 Draw a fin on the fish that is different and colour the other fish.

Description

1 Trace the words **day** and **night**.

2 Colour the daytime pictures.

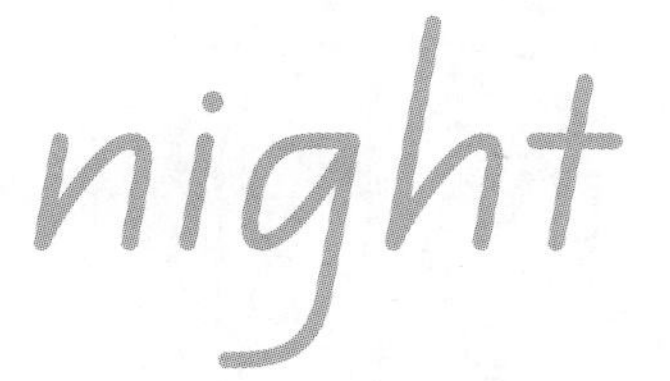

b

d

e

f

Explanation

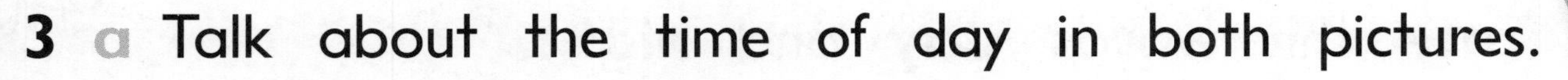

3 a Talk about the time of day in both pictures.

b Colour the daytime picture.

4 a Draw something you do by day and something you do at night.

b Colour both pictures.

Instruction

1 a Trace the numbers.
b Write a telephone number on the lines.

___ ___ ___ ___

___ ___ ___ ___

2 Circle the people who you might talk to on the phone.

Nan Dad Grandpa dog friend

3 Colour the pictures of things you might talk about on the phone.

4 Draw yourself talking to Mum or Dad on the phone.

Writing

5 a Trace **hello**.

b Write in the speech bubbles what the children are saying to each other.

Instruction

1 Draw a sad face or a happy face in each circle to match the picture.

Direction

2 Draw a hat for each happy child.

3 Colour the hats of the clowns that are sad.

4 Draw a tail on each of the happy pigs, then colour your favourite pictures.

Identification

1 Colour the correct picture in each box.

2 Read the sentence, trace **boy** and draw a picture of a boy.

I am a boy.

Association

1 Talk about the story of each book.

2 Colour the objects that belong in each book.

3 Give each book a name.

Description

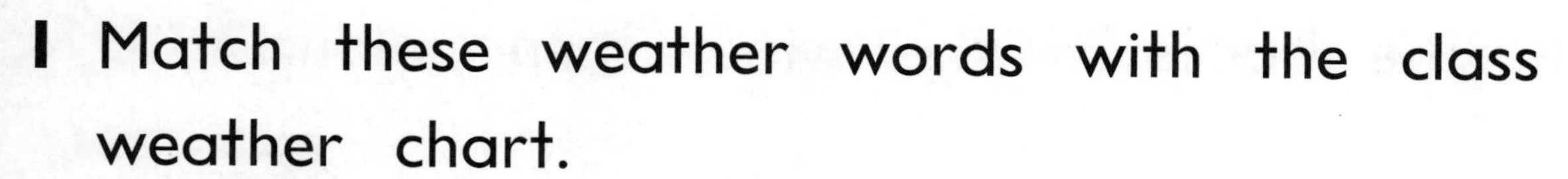

1 Match these weather words with the class weather chart.

2 Write the words under each picture.
Colour the pictures.

Word bank Windy Raining Cloudy Sunny

a ___ ___ ___ ___ ___

b ___ ___ ___ ___ ___ ___ ___

c ___ ___ ___ ___ ___ ___

d ___ ___ ___ ___ ___

Description

3 Circle the boats in the wind, then colour.

a 

b 

c 

4 Colour the birds in the rain.

a 

b 

c 

5 Draw another sheep in the cloudy day pictures.

a 

b 

c 

Association

1 Name all the objects.
2 Circle an object in each set that goes with the picture in the box.

a

b

c

d

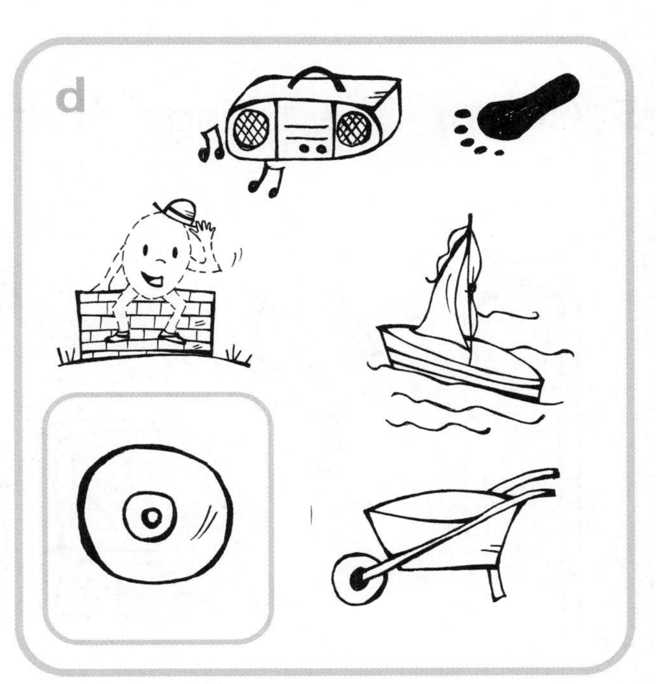

Concepts

3 a Talk about something you lost.

b Colour the place where the key can be found.

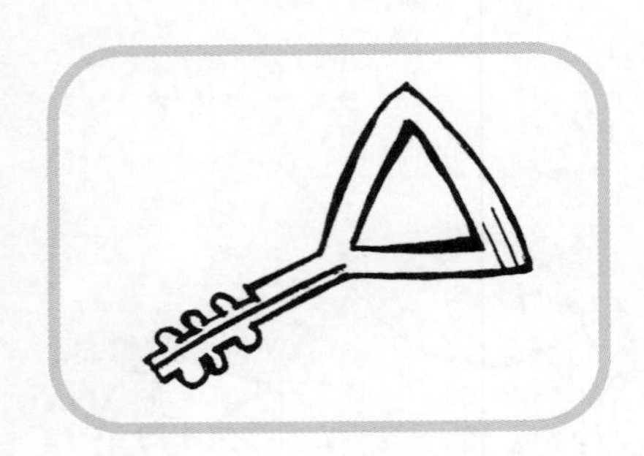

4 Trace **key**, then draw a key.

key

5 Colour the things that need a key.

Instruction

1 Colour all the things that are wrong in this picture.

Instruction

2 Colour the things you can find in the water.

3 Trace the word **fish**, then draw two fish.

fish

Prediction

1 a Talk about the pictures.

b Read the words.

Here is a fire engine.

Where is the fire engine going?

2 a Where are the fire-fighters going?

Tick the **Yes** or **No** boxes.

b Draw the fire-fighters fighting the fire.

... to the library?

Yes  No

... to a bush fire?

Yes  No

Prediction

1 a Discuss games children in wheelchairs can play.
b Colour the pictures.

It is Sports Day.

I am in the race.

2 How will the girl play? Tick the correct picture.
3 Draw children running in the pictures.

I cannot run.

My teacher will help.

Classification

I Colour the pictures in each row that belong to each story.

a

The Three Bears

b

Red Riding Hood

c

Three Little Pigs

Sequence

1 Order these pictures by numbering the boxes 1 – 4.

2 a Colour the boy blue and the haystack yellow.
  b Draw a lamb with the sheep and a tree near the cows.

a

b

c

d

Selection

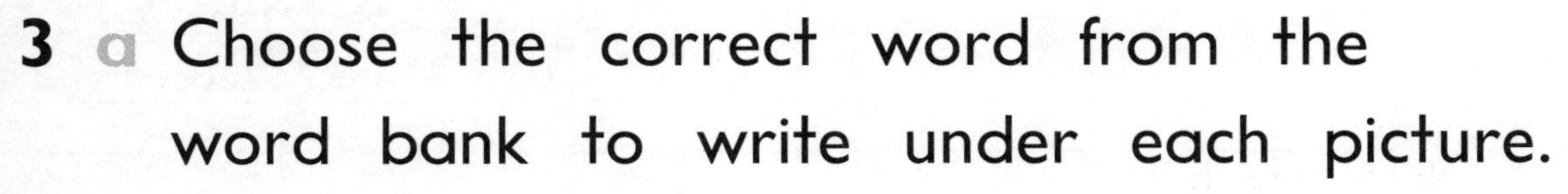

3 a Choose the correct word from the word bank to write under each picture.

b Underline all the rhyming words.

sheep
bee
asleep
tree

boy
row
Roy
toy

sheep
shed
ship
shout

Student Profile

An important part of any teaching program is evaluation. Students need the following skills and strategies in order to achieve success in the early stages of reading. This profile reflects what the student has achieved.

Skills	Assessment	
	Term 1 and 2	Term 3 and 4
Understanding text:		
makes use of: picture clues		
word clues		
sentence clues		
phrase clues		
Uses contextual information		
Makes decisions based on text		
Knows letter clusters make words		
Understands directional conventions		
Develops directional conventions		
Prediction		
uses: picture clues		
word clues		
Cloze activities:		
reads pictures as part of a story		
includes content word from word bank		
Questioning:		
gives answers based on known concepts		
has ability to write a word answer		
develops skill to recall events		
Sequencing skills:		
understands and uses lexical grouping		
understands spacing between words		
follows writing conventions and procedures		
Meaning:		
understands base words		
matches words and pictures		
makes inferences from text		
matches words and meaning		
understands directions		
uses imagination		
relates to personal experiences		
Dictionary skills:		
has knowledge of alphabet		
understands ordering of alphabet		
Writing genre:		
has ability to write: narrative		
poetry		
recount		
description		
Outcomes:		
enjoys reading, writing and is gaining confidence		
understands relationship between spoken and written word		

Answers

UNIT 1 LEGS
1 a echidna, koala, wombat
b emu, kookaburra, duck
c shark, worm, snake
d octopus, jelly fish, grub

UNIT 2 WHAT'S MISSING?
1 a Teacher/parent
2 a wing b paw c eye d tail
e legs f door g hand h kite

UNIT 3 HUMPTY DUMPTY
1 Teacher/parent
2 a yes b no c yes
3 a 4th King b 2nd Humpty

UNIT 4 SOUNDS
1 flowers 2 lizard
3 apple 4 moon

UNIT 5 READING
1 Teacher/parent
2 Teacher/parent

UNIT 6 FAMILY
1 Teacher/parent
2 a My Mum is big. b My cat is little.
3 Teacher/parent

UNIT 7 ALPHABET/NAMES
1 Teacher/parent. 2 Teacher/parent

UNIT 8 LIVING, NON-LIVING
1 a snake, kookaburra, tree, sheep, fish
b guitar, sign, car, gate, television

UNIT 9 HEY DIDDLE DIDDLE
1 d, a, b, c
2 a Teacher/parent b cow, dog, dish, cat

UNIT 10 THE KITCHEN
1 a Teacher/parent
b Teacher/parent

UNIT 11 SAFETY
1 a Teacher/parent
b pot, kettle, toaster, iron, coffee, urn

UNIT 12 COLOURS
1 b rose, fire engine, apple, strawberry (answers may vary)
2 b lemon, banana, daisy, egg (yolk), (answers may vary)

UNIT 13 OBJECTS
1 a bucket b snail
c insect d fish

UNIT 14 SEASONS
1 Teacher/parent
2 a Autumn b Teacher/parent
3 a Winter b Teacher/parent

UNIT 15 THE SENSES – TOUCH
1 coffee, iron, pie, tap (hot)
2 snowman, fridge, ice block, ice water
3 banana, flower, worm, sheep
4 scissors, shells, tooth, truck

UNIT 16 WORDS
1 a Teacher/parent b Teacher/parent
2 a A dog runs to Dad. b Teacher/parent
3 a She is a little girl. b Teacher/parent

UNIT 17 THE GINGERBREAD MAN
1 Teacher/parent 2 Teacher/parent
3 dog, cow, fox 4 Teacher/parent

UNIT 18 PARTY TIME
1 Teacher/parent
2 Teacher/parent (answers may vary)
3 Teacher/parent (answers may vary)

UNIT 19 PAINTING THE HOUSE
Teacher/parent

UNIT 20 FRUIT
1 a cherries, apple, strawberry
b banana, lemon
c grapes, pear, apple (answers may vary)
2 Teacher/parent

UNIT 21 RHYMING WORDS
1 a dice, mice, hose b mice, dice
toe, tree, three tree, three
sun, mum, run sun, run

UNIT 22 ANIMALS
1 snail, tortoise, grub
2 kangaroo, emu, tiger
3 leopard, giraffe, dog
4 snake, zebra, fish
5 slow: turtle; quick: tiger, emu, dog
6 cat, cow, camel

UNIT 23 THREE BLIND MICE/BAA BAA BLACK SHEEP
1 b, d, a, c
2 Teacher/parent
3 b, d, a, c
4 Teacher/parent
5 Teacher/parent
6 a I am the farmer. b I am the black sheep.
c I am the little boy. d I am the dame.

UNIT 24 CLOTHES
1 a shoe b shirt
c glove d sock

UNIT 25 ON THE GRASS
1 Teacher/parent

UNIT 26 POSITION
1 a a – h, b – j, c – f, d – i, e – g
2 Teacher/parent

UNIT 27 CAR TRIPS
1 Teacher/parent (answers may vary)
2 Teacher/parent

UNIT 28 HICKORY DICKORY DOCK
1 b, c, a
2 A mouse ran up the clock.

UNIT 29 UP AND DOWN
1 painter – ladder, lady – escalator, koala – tree, mountain climber – mountain
2 leopard, grub, beetle, lizard

Answers

UNIT 30 BIRTHDAYS
1–2 Teacher/parent

UNIT 31 WORDS AND PICTURES
1 a pig b girl
c car d child running
2 Teacher/parent

UNIT 32 SPRING
Teacher/parent

UNIT 33 WHAT ARE THEY GOING TO DO?/ WHERE ARE THEY GOING?
1 a surfing b going for a walk
c hanging up washing d making snowman
2 Teacher/parent
3 a The boy is running for a bus.
b The girl is going to school.
c The boy is going to bed.

UNIT 34 THE LITTLE RED HEN
1 Teacher/parent
2 c, a, d, b
3 No boxes ticked, as no one helped her
4 Teacher/parent

UNIT 35 TRANSPORT
1 a racing car, car, truck
b rocket, submarine, plane (engines) or parachute, rocket, plane (fly)
c speed boat, row boat, sail boat
2 Teacher/parent
3 a jet, van, car, train, bus, boat
b All except boat have wheels
4 Teacher/parent

UNIT 36 COLOURS
1 a potato, sultanas, worm
b egg (yolk)
c knife and fork, taps
d broccoli, grass, tree
2 Teacher/parent
3 Teacher/parent

UNIT 37 DUCKS
1 Teacher/parent 2 Teacher/parent
3 1, 3 and 4 are the same
4 1 is different

UNIT 38 TIME
1 day – night
2 b, c, e
3 a Teacher/parent b Going to school
4 Teacher/parent

UNIT 39 TELEPHONES
1 Teacher/parent 2 Teacher/parent
3 Teacher/parent 4 Teacher/parent
5 Teacher/parent

UNIT 40 FEELINGS
1 happy – a, b, c, e
2 hats on face 1 and 3
3 coloured 1 and 4
4 tails on 2 and 3

UNIT 41 WORDS
1 a cat b bus
c boy d big
2 Teacher/parent

UNIT 42 BOOKS
1 Teacher/parent
2 a frog, crab, hippopotamus
b gold, Jack, bean stalk
c three trains
d fish with three babies, mouse with three babies
3 Teacher/parent

UNIT 43 WEATHER
1 Teacher/parent
2 a windy b raining
c cloudy d sunny
3 b, c
4 a, b
5 a, c

UNIT 44 AT HOME
1 Teacher/parent
2 a door b baby c mouse d stereo
3 a Teacher/parent
b on chest of drawers
4 Teacher/parent
5 clock, lock, house, car

UNIT 45 FISHING
1 Teacher/parent
2 shark, platypus, jellyfish, seahorse
3 Teacher/parent

UNIT 46 THE FIRE ENGINE
1 Teacher/parent
2 library – no; bushfire – yes

UNIT 47 THE RACE
1 Teacher/parent
2 Teacher will help push.
3 Teacher/parent

UNIT 48 TRADITIONAL STORIES
1 a Goldilocks eats porridge, breaks chair, runs away
b Dancing, knocking on door, putting Grandma in cupboard
c Brick house, knocking on door, stick house

UNIT 49 LITTLE BOY BLUE
1 a c, d, a, b
2 a Teacher/parent
b Teacher/parent
3 a asleep, sheep, tree, Roy, toy, boy, shed, ship, sheep
b asleep, sheep/Roy, toy, boy